BEHIND THE CLOUDS

Understanding the way
of the wholesomeness God

TAIWO ROTIMI

Taiwo Rotimi Copy right 2009

All rights reserved

No part of this publication may be reproduced, stored in a retrievable system, or transmitted in any form or by any means, electronic, mechanical, photocopying, recording or otherwise without the prior permission of the copyright owner.

British Library in Publication Data
A Record of this publication is available
From the British Library

ISBN - 978-0-9561557-0-2

Published by

Platinum Consolidated Publishers
Melbourne Centre
Melbourne Road
Leicester
LE2 0GU
United Kingdom

Website: www.platinumcon.com
Email:behindtheclouds@platinumcon.com

Dedication

The book is dedicated to my immediate family members: Omotola my darling wife; Seyifunmi and Feyisayo, my loving daughters; and Ayomikun, my dearest son, for their understanding, dedication and, most importantly, for believing in me. I love you all.

Acknowledgement

I acknowledge God the Father, the Creator of Heaven and Earth; God the Son, from whom deliverance and redemption of sin came; God the Holy Spirit, coming from both the Father and the Son.

Introduction

Behind the Clouds is a compendium of my personal reaction to the greatness of the Almighty God in creation. In probing the mightiness of Jehovah, there is no gainsaying that there is none like God. One cannot but marvel at the creativity and ingenuity of the Wholesome God.

The book is divided into two parts. The first part discusses the constant moral issues of the world, including freedom, stress, success, human nature, reflection, cruelty, regret, "seven keys to successful living" and many more. The second part deals with the spiritual issues such as the Holy Spirit, The Crucifix, Call to Worship, The Word, Meditation, The Regenerated, Angels, Holy Communion, Spring time etc.

The strong link between the two is the obvious fact that man is made of a body, soul and spirit which co-exist from the time of creation until death when the mortal body and the soul will give way to decay and the spirit will go back to the Eternal One behind the Clouds.

Foreword

I know Taiwo Rotimi to be an effective worker, a thinker and a dedicated minister of God. He always throws himself into any tasks given him. I am not particularly surprised that he has put together this resource material of timeless value on the science of life.

It takes a deep mind to produce a deep book like this; which I will like to refer to as the "contemporary psalms."

Life is a mystery; many merely exist; only a few are truly living. It takes very deep search, unusual understanding, striking insight and outstanding revelation to comprehend its full meaning.

The almightiness of Jehovah cannot be completely fathomed with the mortal mind. What we know and understand are those things which God has revealed to us. It takes a thirsty mind to consciously and deliberately go in search of revelations.

Rotimi has shown through this book that he has a teachable spirit with a broad mind able to assimilate great mysteries. He has consciously gone in search of the force behind the events of life and living with perhaps the motive of helping resolve the inner struggles of many.

This compilation is thought-provoking and reflective. *Behind the Clouds* is necessary for daily meditations and reflections. It is packed with inspirational and easily digested issues, ideals, ideas, anecdotes, experiences, studies and discoveries designed for persons who are eager to get the most out of life.

You have in your hands the technical manual for the science of life. As you read, think, take notes, meditate and then act on the wisdom behind the writings of this timeless resource book, you will be ready to live life to the fullest.

You are about to take a journey behind the clouds; for there exists the Power that makes things work out successfully here and yonder. Your encounter with the mind of God will make you outstanding, anyday, anywhere. Enjoy the journey!

Rev. (Dr) J. S. A. Oladele
General Overseer
The City of the Lord Church
(Formerly C.P.P.C)
Worldwide

Prologue

Behind the Clouds provides readers with a thorough and insightful introduction to the sacredness of the Eternal Spirit behind the clouds, through whom all things were commanded to be.

In probing the might and wholesomeness of Jah Jehovah, the poet's adoption of simple yet instructive language in his investigation, report and recommendation make *Behind the Clouds* a prescription for all ailments.

Rotimi leads readers gently into the unfathomable depth of the Creator's love for humanity, healing for the sick, strength for the weak, freedom for the captives, succour for the hopeless and power for those who diligently seek His face.

Behind the Clouds is a prescription for healthy living. Please remember to take it.

Behind the Clouds is a book that endeavours to discern the Ageless Power operating behind the Universe

BEHIND THE CLOUDS

THE GOD OF CREATION

Contents

Part I

1. Freedom	21
2. Am I Stressed?	23
3. A Champion	24
4. Human Nature	25
5. Are you ready?	27
6. The Gatherer	29
7. Everlasting Love	30
8. The Moon	31
9. Ask, Believe, Receive	32
10. My Darling	33
11. Life's Challenges	35
12. Success	36
13. To God be the Glory	38
14. My Special Friend	39
15. Simplicity	41
16. Reflect	42
17. The Reality	43
18. The Fearless	44
19. The Regret	45
20. Forgiveness	46
21. The Seven Keys to Successful Living	47

Part II

1. Behind the Clouds	49
2. The Good News	50
3. Resurrection	52
4. Thankfulness	54
5. Revelation	55
6. My Father	57
7. The Word	58
8. Call to Worship	59
9. Purify your body	60
10. Let's Celebrate	61
11. The Crucifix	62
12. The Covenant	64
13. Hour of Prayer	65
14. The Call	67
15. The Holy One	68
16. Armageddon	69
17. Carry Your Cross	70
18. My Guardian Angel	71
19. The Regenerated	73
20. The Holy Spirit	74
21. Adoption	76
22. One Happy Family	78
23. Image of God	79
24. Immortality	81
25. Obedience	82
26. Sanctification	83
27. Evangelise	84
28. Guilty	85
29. My Peace	86
30. New Beginning	88
31. It's Spring Time	90
32. Call Me	91
33. My Plan for You	93
34. Go for It	94

35. The Judgment	96
36. Holy Communion	98
37. Your Mindset	100
38. Dead Branch	102
39. His Gifting	106
40. Fulfilled Life	108
41. A Good Friendship	110
42. Use Me	112
43. Guide Me	113
44. Faithful Saviour	114
45. Fill Me O Lord	115
46. Your Disciple	116
47. Your loving arms	117
48. What is Life	118
49. I will make Heaven	120
50. Epilogue	123

Graphic illustrations

Part I

1. Freedom 22
2. Am I stressed 23
3. Human nature 26
4. Everlasting Love 30
5. The Moon 31
6. My Darling 34
7. Success 37
8. My Special Friend 40
9. Simplicity 41
10. Reflect 42
11. Reality 43
12. Fearless 44
13. The Regret 45
14. Forgiveness 46
15. The Seven Keys of Life 47

Part II

1. Behind the Clouds 49
2. Resurrection 53
3. Thankfulness 54
4. Revelation 56
5. My Father 57
6. The Word 58
7. Let's Celebrate 61
8. The Crucifix 63
9. Armageddon 69
10. Carry Your Cross 70
11. My Guardian Angels 72
12. The Regenerated 73
13. The Holy Spirit 75
14. Image of God 80

15. Immortality — 81
16. Sanctification — 83
17. My Peace — 87
18. It's Spring Time — 90
19. My Plan — 93
20. Go for It — 95
21. Judgment — 97
22. Holy Communion — 99
23. Your Mindset — 101
24. A Dead Branch — 105
25. A Fulfilled Life — 109
26. A Good Friendship — 111
27. What is Life — 119
28. I Will Make Heaven — 121

Last book by the Author

Lighting Shadow is written to mark the Bi-Centenary of the Abolition Charter of the Trans-Atlantic Slave Trade 1807- 2007

For your Books order:

Lighting Shadow by Taiwo Rotimi

Behind the Clouds by Taiwo Rotimi

Please log on to:

Email:www.platinumcon.com

Email:www.nigershowbiz.com

Email:lightingshadow@platinumcon.com

Email: behindtheclouds@platinumcon.com

Write to:

Platinum Consolidated Publishers

Suite 20

Melbourne Centre

Melbourne Road

Leicester

LE2 0GU

United Kingdom

We remember 1807 - 2007

I say:

peace and love

to all mankind,

slavers and slaves

human and de-humanised

history:

had already pronounced its judgment.

That's why!

we remember them today as always

their memories, we cannot forget

even if we want to

we shall tell the true unending story

 to the children in the womb

But, we've forgiven them.

We remember: But we've forgiven them

BEHIND THE CLOUDS

PART ONE

Freedom

How free
Is he that you set free
from bondage, sorrow, affliction,
evil, temptations
5   hands in shackles he dreams of no more
'cause he's set free at last

How independent
Is he from curse of generational sins
fragrance of sanction in hell fire,
10 will he smell not again
'cause he was born,
to be redeemed

How peaceful
Is he walking down the aisle
15 worry, fear and frustration
are but moving shadows to be melted away
storming wind of sleepless nights no more
'cause he's finally released

How blessed
20 Is he with Abraham's generational blessings
promised through the special blood
free from condemnation and inherited curses,

the seventy-years life span
holds him captive no more
25 'Cause he's destined to live for ever.

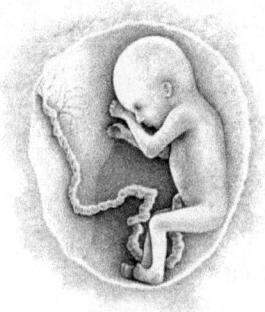

Freedom: Destined to live for ever

Am I Stressed?

My past is history
tomorrow can wait for its turn
the reality of my history
Is today the antecedent of my tomorrow?
am I stressed?

Think of nothing; happy moments
look back to glorious days
of laughter and joy
liberated music; effective tonic for longevity
tell me, am I stressed?

Self prophetic affirmations of good fortune
love and services to humanity in my thoughts
will meditate in the morning and at bedtime
throw depression out of my windows
please tell me, am I stressed?

No pity of the past, or frustration of today
will work and walk and inhale fresh air
drive out poisonous fumes from my system
will not think yesterday or fret tomorrow
Now know, I'm not stressed.

Stressed: I am not stressed

A Champion

Failure
not a friend
blame nobody or something
neither should you give up

5   No illogical reasoning or behaviour
drunkenness, or suicide,
nervous breakdown, not your portion
no deception, no apology

Failure
10   should it becloud your judgement?
can it hijack your plans?
your past shortcomings are gone forever

Seize every opportunity that comes your way
no procrastination, no speculation
15   face your challenge squarely
make it a stool for your greatness

Accept your faults, and move on
realistically, truthfully and honestly
20   befriending failure is like giving up
certainly not your intention

A winner does not quit, a quitter does not win
You are a Champion.

The Human Nature

Man;
body, soul and spirit
body; a casket for decay
soul; the mind, emotion and will
spirit returns to its source

Bodily showcase
floating earthly vessel
heartily soul
life wire voltage
power house of the spiritual consciousness

No matter what
life like beautiful flowers
blossom in day light
soon wither and rot away at midnight
back to the earth; its source

Spiritual home
resides with the Owner
hell for an evil doer
heaven for the good doer
on Judgement Day

Death
never an avoidable end
the transformation footpath
that leads to the Giver
Lord, God, Almighty

Death
never a life's terminator
rather the genesis and revelation
of every single small part

30   That completes a unified whole.

The Human Nature: Beautiful, so temporal

Are You Ready?

And when the battle is won
chariots of war perished
death stood on the highway,
to welcome the victors
5   to heaven, their home

A guest you are
special guest of the world
shall return some day
to heaven,
10 your home

To heaven
where no pain resides
in the heavenly home
no night or darkness
15 home of peace and tranquility

Are you ready?
to go now
before the arrow of death
pierces through your hearts
20 like knife cutting through butter

At home
no darkness, no dizziness
no noise or silence
no fear no hope
25 but eternal joy

In heaven your home
life, hope and love
joy consumes sorrow

life wallops death
30 Holy, Holy, Holy the redemption song.

The Gatherer

Chasing after shadow that is external
leaving the substance that is internal
laugh from their mouth and not their heart
talk flippantly and not constructively
vow without any fulfilment
walk in darkness of day night
eat gluttonously and vomit iniquities
excrete impurities and indignation
heart full of evil and immoralities
soul mortgaged to
the Prince of Darkness
they gather, gather and gather more
more than their generation would ever need
Have an idea who will take them home.

The Everlasting Love

A new love, unblemished and pure
like a new baby is heavenly made
to be delivered on Earth
an alien is it?
5   a bundle of joy to the world
not only to the favoured couples
but also to the well wishers

Love
sweet love
10   bond between God and Man
upright Angels
singing Hallelujah in worshipping the Father,
they remind us
of Father's abiding love.

15   No matter the set back
despite the set up
not minding the pain and frustration
afflictions, sickness, verdicts and debts
no matter the circumstances,
20   they do not affect His unconditional love
For mankind.

The Everlasting Love: Pure, Unblemished

The Moon

Moon,
the beautiful Queen of the night
permanently beaming with smiles
lighting away the darkness
of their inner mind

Ever grateful for your smiles
illumination of darkness
with the Queen up there
fear has no stronghold
over the little ones down here
running about in the beautiful night
playing, laughing, shouting
singing the night away
under your cover and protection
their voices heard miles away.

Children seated with the village elders
passing on the tales and wisdom
under the Queen's supernatural gift
To mankind.

The Moon: Queen of the night

Ask, Believe, Receive

Design a solitary place
to be alone
make sure of your needs
write them down for better understanding
ask without fear or doubt
adopt positive and affirmative words
believe they have been achieved
close your eyes, visualize them
see them, touch them, confess them

Be thankful
and celebrate them
be cool, be humble, be in control
keep your faith hat on at all times
Give to humanity the benefits.

My Darling

To hold and love
to cherish and adore
to honour and care for
my darling wife
to honour and care for
to obey and respect
to love and cherish
my darling husband

In difficult situations
shall not forsake thee
in a happy moment
will always be by your side
in sickness and in health,
in wealth and poverty
will not abandon you

In bareness and abundance,
in celebration and trials,
in peace and confusion,
we shall not blame one another,
closer than before we shall be

We would learn to forgive and forget,
we are not only to honour one another,
trust; the foundation of our love,
will strengthen our resolve in each other
our love will see us through

Running away from trials and temptations,
calling each other obscene names,
like looking back to yesterday,
increases heartaches and high blood pressure,
brings no solutions or respite

To hold and love
to cherish and adore
in a happy moment
In difficult situations
our compassion will see us through

To look back is to be damned
mistakes are like learning curves,
must be made and learned from
for our world to complete its circle,
must learn fast and quickly too
when focused to be a success
All is well.

My Darling: Two hearts as one

Life's Challenges

They come
suddenly to man
when everything seems winding and tortuous
everyone seems deaf and so far away
from the shout for help

Better tomorrow
seems a mirage; tarry for ever
would it ever come?
open-ended question begging for an answer
friends and helpers, vanished,
family turns jesters and unreachable,
foes close by, giggling and whispering

Reproach, shame, debt, curse, pain
anxiety, ill health, conspired together
with thought of suicide,
as easy as abc
to end it all

After a stormy night
comes a sunshine day
finally, the darker night slips away forever
but only for those who can endure to the end
new thoughts with rekindled hope
windows of opportunity suddenly open
Welcome to the world of realities.

Success

To be successful
is to be on top
are you a cab driver, a rubbish collector?
do the societal paradigms
see you as nobody?

If you pursue
life of greed, lawlessness and brutality
throw away your humanity
and still stay on top
will your conscience be at rest?

Is it inherent in man
to be reckless, brutal and selfish,
for wealth, position and status?
If honestly poor
are you a failure?

To maim, destroy and kill
for man's inordinate ambition
what does it matter, and who cares?
so long as you belong
the end justifies the means, so it seems

Will you ever enjoy your wealth?
should your heart be at rest?
why should you live at peace?
with deceit, cheat, lies, wickedness?
O Lord! Have mercy

Vanity upon vanity,
what does it profit a man
he that sows deceitfully
do unto others

30   Father, forgive them

        To be successful
        discover His plan for your life
        progress and everlasting happiness
        already in His plans for you
35   find out without any shortcuts

        Your life will not be cut short
37   But at peace with man and God.

Success: Congratulations

To God Be the Glory

More precious than gold
worth more than silver
never to be wasted or wished away
time wisely spent together
5   in peace and harmony

In good thoughts and positive deeds
soothing and actively lived happy moments
in saying thank you for a wonderful moment
to God be the Glory
10   not in bitterness anger or regret

What happened has happened
Peace made; the damage done
good memory or a sober reflection
generate memories not regrets

15   To God be the Glory
your response to events is what matters
it will either mar or make you
A word is enough for the wise.

My Special Friend

Part One

You are my friend,
a special part of me
more concerned about my well being
thanks for being
a special part of me
you are my special friend
through all seasons of life

Part Two

You are my friend,
not afraid to be frank with the truth
not ashamed to be naked with me
laughed off our idiosyncrasies
cried together in our sorrowful moments
held nothing back from each other
we are meant for each other

Part Three

You are my special friend,
no pretences, suspicions or emotion overplayed
or underplayed
no lying, cheating, or teasing
poured out our emotion without holding back

trusting, loving and devoted to each other
appreciating one another
and thanking God
For such a special friendship.

My Special Friend: Together for ever

Simplicity

Buy for utility's sake
not for impression
buy, be addicted not
to nothing for nothing
give to the poor, the needy
in your society

Shun the spirit of covetousness
restrict your assertive nature
thank God more for His blessings
enjoy life without regret
stop blaming the past

Run, run, run away from obsession
the first cousin of addiction
never mortgage your present for the future
there's still hope for a life
bruised, maligned and restricted

Refuse to surrender to the sinful nature
oppression, exploitation, and obscenity
run, run, run away from them
be loyal, be honest, be truthful
Be natural, be open, be simple.

Simplicity: Gently and Easy

Reflect

Reflect;
don't study
let go;
never hold on,
just stop, don't run

Righteousness not through self
see me dwell in the shadow of the Messiah
passing through the valley of death
evil shall fear me
I shall not be dumbfounded
neither will I be confounded
for He is my strength and shield

Will hear Him and obey Him,
worshipping Him, honouring Him,
not as a religious act
a way of life that commands full obedience
on my part

Study and reflect on His word
Let go and not hold on tight.

Reflect: Don't just think

The Reality

The law of reality
constant and unambiguously expressed
the more man wrestles with it
the more frustrating, irrational he becomes
5   harder he tries to fight it
weaker and inconsequential he gets

It's good to
unwind, relax and unassuming
as situation folds and unfolding
10 to be untangled and tangled

Eternity and death
accomplished not by self justification
with life's pain and anxiety
a closed door somewhere
15 leads to a wider pathway elsewhere

To accept reality
of pain, separation, sorrow and death
we lessen our reaction to negativity
enhance and open up to positive vibes
20 Essential for growth, peaceful co-existence.

The Reality: Life is real

Fearless

Man
should accept what comes to him
worry not, fear less
accept what comes your way with dignity
5   chart not what comes not
do not let your talents rust away
be cool and calculating
your dull moment will soon be passed over

Life's
10 full of contradictions and complexities
what does not come matters less
what is in your grasp
may not mean much to you now
Must be securely kept and guided.

Fearless: Courage to take a decision

The Regret

How he wished
things were seen differently
spent time more frugally
treated people with more respect
used time more prudently
how he wished,
to turn back the hands of the clock
wasted on nothingness

How he wished
could not have wished to wish
to have seen life differently
be more compassionate
spent quality time with the sick and helpless,
But loved God more.

The Regret: Inseparable with time

Forgiveness

To undo the past
trust that was misplaced
misfortune that was caused
accounts that were mismanaged
5   lies blatantly fabricated
opportunities deliberately bungled
false witness hurriedly put together
promises never kept
hearts broken
10 depression caused

Repent, confess and restitute,
He's ready, willing and able
to cleanse you from all grubbiness
Make you whole again.

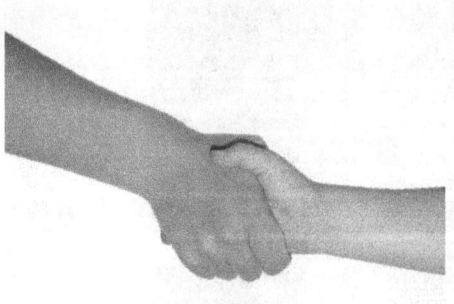

Forgiveness: Brings peace of mind

The Seven Keys of Life

There are many keys
to unlock the door of success
only seven I know of
can truly open the door:
5   humble yourself for honours,
guide and guard your utterances
be moderate in your thought and action
practise love, show gratitude for little things
let go of anger and anxiety
10   allow in the air of forgiveness
money is good but cannot buy everything
be at peace with self and fellowmen
life will be lived fully
To its fullest.

The Seven Keys of Life: Solution for Man

BEHIND THE CLOUDS

PART TWO

Behind the Clouds

Let's go deeper and deeper
inside the deep end
heavy stuff of unusual level
things superior and supernatural
5   from trivialities to serious matters
mundane to spiritual
intangibilities to tangibles

Let's probe the beginning
the beginning of our very existence
10   existence of the essence of our being
being; the Apple of God's eye.

Behind the Clouds: In the shekhinah of God

The Good News

      Goodness and mercy of the Good News
      shall follow you
      all the days of your life
      in the land of the living
5   you shall possess your possessions

      The Seed of the Virgin
      foreknew before creation
      the Seed;
      redeemed man
10   from sanctions of the law

      The Good News not a surprise one
      for God Almighty
      always show signs and wonders
      His mysteries are only for the initiated
15   but His call is for all

      Yahweh;
      needs no avenger for His course
      All Mighty, All Powerful, All Sufficient
      will fight His own battles
20   needs no help from mortals

      His Good News
      full of goodness to all men
      His birth;
      a hidden mystery to the uninitiated
25   yet an education to the world

      The Rabbi and Elders
      acknowledged the Master at the Temple
      Giver of wisdom and understanding,
30   Earth trembled when He spoke

The Good News brought
hope to the hopeless
liberty to the captives
abundant wealth to the impoverished

35 Beautiful garments to the naked
Bread of life to the hungry
good life to the dying
shining light; to the dark world

40 the sick, healed
the lost, found
the weak regained their strength

Born for man
not to die again but to live forever
45 to be united with his Maker
to regain the lost fellowship
but this time
For eternity.

Resurrection

    From the beginning
    Son of Man knew
    He would be persecuted
    nailed to the bitter cross
5   buried in the belly of the Earth for three days

    Son of Man knew,
    He would rise up on the third day
    Earth, had no hold over Him
    the Oracles have spoken
10   the message is for eternity

    For Him,
    to have died without resurrection,
    Christianity becomes a non-Living faith,
    nothing to live or hope for
15   darkness would have been glorified

    Because, He rose again,
    everlasting peace swallowed eternal chaos
    power of darkness, illness and bareness
    buried there in the Earth
20   the Master has risen up

    His Resurrection Power,
    to be experienced personally
    do not let it slip you by
    sin no more
25   be resurrected with Him

    Sting of death for a sinful nature
    His blood; atonement
    for remission of sin
    freedom on a platter of gold

30   for Mankind

To die,
to the lust of sin
to experience the impossibilities
with no restriction to colour, race or creed
35   resurrection brought total redemption

Freedom to the Saints in bondage,
obedience by mortals
deliverance to true worshippers
who worship in Spirit and in Truth
40   freedom from reproach and damnation

Died,
to set the captives free
free forever
forever, for man to make the choice
choice to be free
45   Free forever.

Resurrection: He is risen

Thankfulness

Thank Him
for what He has done
appreciate what He's doing right now
gratitude for what He'll do next
5   bless Him for what He's yet to do

The spirit of thankfulness
always dwell in your soul
be thankful
if to unlock the key to His grace and favour
10 grateful hearts worship, praise and adore Him
in everything and with everything
as long as you have breath
will ever remain thankful
For His loving kindness and faithfulness.

Thankfulness: The receptive heart

Revelation

My Father said,
let there be Light
and there was Light
since that day
5   darkness comprehended it no more

My Mentor said,
I am the Gate the only Gate
since then
gates of darkness
10   barred His children no more

My friend said,
call me by my Pseudo-name
I will spontaneously come
since then
15   all other names are inconsequential

My Lord said to me,
I am He that I am
The Beginning and the End
since then
20   all other forces are powerless

Awesome and Wholesome God He is,
The Holy of Holies, Originator,
Navigator, Motivator, Generator,
Provider, Defender, Challenger,
25   Deliverer, Comforter, Restorer

All Mighty, All Powerful, All Faithful

An Ever-Sure God of Creation.

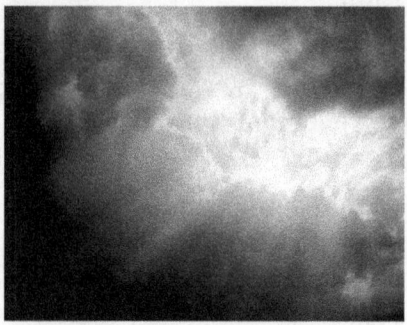

Revelation: Only to the gifted

My Father

If He says something
It shall surely come to pass

He's the Almighty God
5   Other gods are nothing
If He promises
He never fails

He's not a man
That He should lie
10 He does not need repentance

He's all powerful and able
He never fails
If He says yes
Nobody can say no.

My Father: Who art in Heaven

The Word

      I'll study your Word
      steadfastly with prayers,
      will meditate in them
      sincerely and in fasting
5   powerfully and sequentially I will go through
      with help from
      You; dear Holy Spirit

      The understanding of your Word
      is my ultimate goal,
10   a living example of your Word
      a shining light to others
      unending pot of oil
      a double-edged sword
      Light to my feet.

The Word: A lamp unto my feet

Call to Worship

He is here
The Father Almighty
Master Creator
we see and feel the works of His hands
His presence in them, undeniable
when I am alone, or in group
Your word is settled for ever
we worship You
Sabbath; Your day of rest
a day of blessing and worship
with full expectations

Your word: a shield and sword
Your testament: for my salvation
nourishment for weary soul
we shall lean on nothing but Your word
gratitudes shall feel the depth of our hearts
our thanks offerings
to You, our Lord, God
from You; Father
Your divine blessings.

Purify Your Body

Your head is anointed with power
guard your eyes from seeing evil
protect your nostrils from bad smell
watch your mouth from blabbing
your ears must be shut to trivialities
protect your anus and hands
your private parts should be private
from all penetrations of evil
remember to cover your whole body
with the blood
not of the lamb, rams and sheep
but the precious blood
of the begotten Son
Of God, Almighty.

Let's Celebrate

O Come,
let's celebrate
God our Maker,
to sing and
make a joyful noise to Him

Sing, clap, dance,
beautifully in His presence
let's jump up and down,
crawl and bend down,

Worshipping the King of Kings,
Lord of Lords, we adore Thee,
let's glorify the Messiah;
our praises, joyful noise, adoration,
for our Lord, God

Glory and honour to
Him in the Highest.

Let's celebrate: Life's celebration

The Crucifix

      You mortified me in vain
      nails, nailed me down
      mourn, 'cause I was crucified?
      lament, for the agony?
5   it is written; what's going to be, is going to be

      Your sentence, my eternity,
      your excruciation, my strength
      your crucifixion, my resurrection
      your cruelty, my loving kindness
10   it is written; what's going to be is going to be

      Sinners must be penitent,
      hate evil, do good
      what did I get?
      Crucify him! Crucify him! Crucify him!
15   O! Forgive them, Father

      Hell, for Satan,
      Heaven, my Father
      fear for Pilate and his Council
      division for the Temple's veils
20   Lightning thunder confirmed my name

      World in great dread,
      to see their Lord transposed
      Hallelujah song heaven filled
      the third day
25   living praised the Living God.

      Ascended unto Heaven,
      seated at God's right hand
      My blood; atonement
      nobody goes to my Father

30   except through me; His only Son

       I am the Way,
       The Water, Shepherd, Spring and the Tree,
       ye that labour and are heavy laden
       come to me, drink from my spring of life
35   I will give you peace.

The Crucifix: Died that man may live

The Covenant

From fellowship
in the Garden of Eden
to worker and labourer in the world
came redemption by the Trinity
5   Grace of God to man
through Christ; the Mediator

Condition of obedience for fellowship
tempted by Satan for knowledge
disobedience brought death and curse
10 to the man god
forfeited fellowship with the Spirit-God
punished with physical and spiritual death
God's grace endures for ever

Grace requires no work justification
15 man is already condemned under the law
justification is only by Faith in the Son
obedience to God's commandments
the price; an eternity with the Father

To be under the covenant of work,
20 is to be circumcised,
to continue is to obey all its
dictates, festivals and ceremonies
baptism is to be under the Grace

Partaking in the Lord's Supper
25 evidence of continuity
till being present at the Lord's table
In His Father's Kingdom.

The Hour of Prayer

Lord,
hear my supplications.
I shall not ask according to my own will
but as Thou wilt
5   with faith,
You, Lord, will not disregard my voice

I shall obey Thy word
confession of sin is mine
remission of sin is Yours
10 I shall forgive those that wronged me

my pride and arrogance
in total humility
I lay them down at your feet
will be devoted, consistent and humble
15 at all times

For Your blessings and favour.
I have learnt to wait upon you, O Father
in the corner of my heart,
20 will remain faithful

In the privacy of my room
shall not look around.
I will call unto Thee,
and You will answer my prayer
25 In supplication with others

We shall tear down forces of darkness
with our weapons of faith
In Your name
comes freedom for the captives
30 peace for the troubled hearts

In Your name
weakness is made strong
inadequacy turned to strength
In Your glory
35   darkness and impossibilities are removed

For answered prayers
we shall honour Your name,
for unanswered prayers,
we shall not lose hope or grow weary

40   The Lord's Prayer of "passing the cup over"
was with caution,
Apostle Paul begged the Father thrice
to remove the thorns
"My grace is sufficient for you" the reply,

45   King David wanted security for Absalom
his prayer was discountenanced,
Martyrs died violent death
Yet they loved not their lives even unto death

Shall not ask according to my will
50   but as Thou wilt
with Faith,
Ye shall hear my weary voice.

The Call

Created by His Majesty,
before the creation;
in the eternal past
those to be called.

5   Not because of work,
but His grace,
not because of merit,
for they've all messed up,
it's for His purpose and good pleasure,
10   vessels for honour

To be called,
is to have been chosen in the distant past,
for His selection,
is to have been nominated,
15   the grace of Christ the Son
is justifiable in God the Father,
attested to by the Holy Spirit
for believers

Why did He call them?
20   'cause they are the chosen ones
the invitation is to all
only those who honoured the call
Are the justifiable ones.

The Holy One

The Holy One,
You have no beginning or end
No ancestor or successor
A Timeless being, an Unchangeable Changer,
5   Eternal King, an Infinite Creator,
The Alpha and Omega,
Immaterial, Independent Father,
The Impassable, Indivisible Trinity,
Omnipotent, Omniscient, Omnipresent One

10 You are ever faithful, and a Perfect Master,
Merciful, Gracious, Patient, a good Father,
The Holiest, Righteous, Most Powerful Lord,
Peaceful, Blessed, Adjudicator,
Ever Transcendent and Glorious King.

15 Dear Father,
You are the One and the only One,
My loving Saviour,
The great Comforter
I worship you,
20 The Triune God

The Armageddon

Sun has its own splendour,
Moon is not without one,
Stars' brightness,
Differ from one and other
5   The dead shall rise again,
The sick receive their healing
Perishable will no longer taste death
Material made spiritual
The weak made powerful
10 Humiliation turns to glorification

After the destruction and death,
Comes judgment,
the wedding of the Lamb
The one thousand year reign of Jesus Christ.

The Armageddon: The End of the beginning

Carry Your Cross

You cannot bribe God
You cannot corrupt Him
You cannot hurry God
You cannot intimidate Him
You cannot lie to God
You cannot limit Him,
You cannot deceive God
You cannot fight Him
You cannot play God
You cannot take His glory

You cannot go on without His love
He loves you and had paid the ultimate price
He left His glorious throne for a lowly shed
You must humble yourself

You cannot live without your cross
He carried His and yours, you must
He had overcome the world and glorified
You too can.

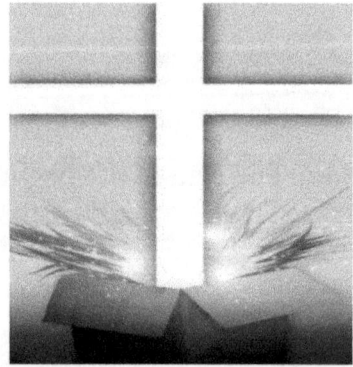

Carry Your Cross: You Must Carry Yours

My Guardian Angel

My dear Guardian Angel
you are a spiritual being
made to live by the Creator

My dear Guardian Angel
your intelligence, power, speed,
far higher, greater than mine
fast, sexless, ageless, sickless, never marry
gifted in many tongues and any form

The Cherubim
Guardians of the Garden of Eden
diligent messengers with the flaming swords

The Seraphim
round the throne of Grace
created solely to worship the Most High God

Angels; are to worship, run errands for Him
never to be worshipped by man
whose total loyalty is to the Creator

My Guardian Angel
though you are faster, more powerful,
more intelligent than I
you are not created in His Image
neither were you made in His Likeness

I will still be your judge at end time
you had better guide me securely
Because I am a small god.

My Guardian Angel: Worship, run errands

The Regenerated

A new life in Christ Jesus
through His saving grace
in faith
believe in Him
you shall be saved
To be regenerated
as evidence of total life change
new body, spirit and soul
old things have passed away
all have become new

Through
the new birth
man is regenerated
One headship with the Trinity.

The Regenerated: New body in Christ

The Holy Spirit

Ultimate Giver of life and power,
Commander of truthfulness,
wisdom and righteousness,
Initiator of hope, joy and love
5   Provider of intelligence, direction, conscience
Unifier, Illuminator and Regenerator

Be ye troubled no more,
trust and rest in the Lord
10   be thankful at all times
be assured by His word

Holy Spirit, heal me,
make me whole
the blood of the Lamb
15   wash away my inherited transgression
cleanse my own iniquities
let me be a living witness of thy glory
let people see and feel Your presence in me

Holy Spirit
20   make me Your Evangelist
grant me Your healing and cleansing power
let me bind and release,
with power to cast out, and heal
remove peoples' hindrances, set them free
25   let the Power of anointing
mightily come on me

Holy Spirit
use me as a vehicle
30   of honour for Your name
my Lord and Shepherd
Father I am here before You

heal me and set me on fire for Your name
at the end of my journey
35   Count me worthy of Your worship.

The Holy Spirit: The voice of the truth

Adoption

A new life,
appointed
to stand before Him
adoption;
5   makes mankind
a member of God's extended family
children of the Father,
heirs of the Kingdom

We are the adopted,
10   let's emulate the Father
to be in love with Him
Daddy is kind, honest and righteous,
so we should be
but if in doubt
15   we are not of Him,
He can't be for us

As brethren,
how can He suffer
and we pray to escape punishments,
20   we must experience suffering and pain
beating, shame, and face death,
for our belief and His name's sake
till the morning of glory comes
when we shall claim the golden crown
25   promised for the Conquerors

We rest our faith in Him,
we can call Him
He will never forsake or leave us,
Abba! Father; because He is love

30	Our Lord Jesus Christ; the firstfruit removes us from the damnation of sin, We fear no evil.

One Happy Family

His personal call
thou must be received
to be born again
clothed in the spiritual garment
of His exemplary life
Is for us to mirror

To share with Him
to stand before His throne of Grace
a member of His family
is to repudiate sins
Trust and confide in Him

Bringing
joy to His chosen children
One united happy family.

The Image of God

Man
in likeness of God,
with dominion, power and authority
over the sea, air, land
all over the Earth

Every creeping thing
all living things
must answer to Man's call

To multiply, fruitful, and dominate
created uniquely
more highly favoured than the Angels

When I consider Thy works in creation,
I marvel at Your ingenuity
In all the Earth and in Heaven
the supernatural status bestowed on man
In the scheme of things
Oh! *Baba,** You are Awesome

You crowned him with Your glory,
You honoured him with Your name,
You placed him above and blessed him,

Ears have not heard,
Eyes have not seen,
What You have prepared for him
In his glory.

Baba: Father

The Image of God: Adam and Eve

Immortality

Mortal,
poor, lowly, weak and sinful nature
receives the gift of immortality
corruptible to incorruptible,
5   perishable; becomes imperishable,
buried in humiliation
but rose up glorified

Spiritually made,
physically delivered
10   The Mighty King in man's clothing
Immortal God of creation,
Immortality; never inborn or inherent in man,
was His right;

through the precious blood of the Lamb
15   flowing from the fountain of the Father's love
to redeem Mankind from the sanction of hell
brought by his disobedience in the garden
to prepare him for eternal fellowship
With Him, the Son and the Holy Spirit.

Immortality: God's nature

Obedience

To obey is non-negotiable
to ask according to His will
is to be pleasing and loving Him
striving for perfection before Him
carrying out His assignments assiduously

Win souls for the Redeemer
bring back disenchanted sheep to the Flock
a good example for others
through the perceived obedience
lost sheep shall be brought back

His wrath is to be avoided
His reward must be sought at all times
relationship with Him will be rewarded
Angels will rejoice at man's good work
glorify the Almighty Father

His peace, joy and happiness
shall dwell in man's life
for following His commands
his life shall not be cut short
Shall live to see his children's children.

Sanctification

To be sanctified
Is to proclaim the flesh
dead to sin
alive in Christ
5   through the power of the Holy Spirit
a continuing exercise
only ends in death
Jesus Christ was sanctified
for His mission on Earth
10   so you must be sanctified

Sanctify me O God
for the power of the Holy Spirit
to live a sinless Christ-like life
Worthy of His glory.

Sanctification: Making anew

Evangelise

Go ye into the world!
declare my Good News
to all mankind without exception
he that hears and believes
is my friend; the redeemed
he that hears and desperate for a drink
will my Spring of life nourish
he that hears and shuns my word
stands condemned already

Go ye my brethren!
Tell it throughout all nations
make disciples of all nations
my second coming will tarry
until the Good News reaches
all corners of the Earth

To free man from excuses and regrets
When I come to reign on Earth.

Guilty

Guilty as charged
death;
punishment for sin
serpent;
you crawled into the world
The dragon:
will be kicked out, at the end
and permanently be destroyed

Satan has been before our creation
kicked out and tossed down to our world
just for a little while
until the Father decides
to end the final conflict
In glory.

My Peace

Peace!
Relief for human soul
desired, and sought after
mul-ti-tudes searched and searched
5   throughout our world
from cre-a-tion to cre-a-tion
couldn't find, purchase or discover it?
can human knowledge, wisdom bequeath it?
can fame behold it
10   No

Peace!
lacked by monks in secluded caves
personality disorder tried it doing drugs
sniffing and in drunk-en-ness
15   in a recluse living
the rich, powerful and the strong
oppressing, and exploiting the weak
yet!
Peace is so far away
20   even in suicide

His Peace!
'cause of love, He gave to all,
The-Prince-of-Peace
lived on;
25   gave His life for a Peace-Per-fect-Peace
left behind;
on His ascension

To His Father
He desires genuine and ever-last-ing peace
30   that hearts shall no more be trou-bled

My Peace!
in the world in your time,
in a position of authority
multiply, fruitful and subdue;

35   I; the loving Father
still waiting, pleading,
at your door,
will enter only if called in
40   to give you my eternal peace

My peace I bring to the world,
My peace I leave with you
Will I find peace when I return?

My Peace: I give you

The New Beginning

      I am doing a new thing
      mouth will be opened wide apart
      tongues will confess,
      the aroma will be pleasing
5.   ears shall stand to attention
      when they hear,
      eyes will be swishing
      to behold
      the supernatural work of my hands
10   the unbelievers
      will stand up and be counted
      on seeing the greatness of Me, Yahweh. Selah

      Downtrodden,
      shall be lifted up high,
15   to my Majestic throne
      the mighty and lords,
      will be brought crashing down
      the weak and the desolate
      will be made strong and honourable
20   sick and the afflicted
      will be healed
      beggar and the reproached
      will lend to nations
      Because I am the Jehovah Jireh. Selah

25   The I Am, That I Am;
      The Beginning and the End
      The Unchangeable Changer

      The Lord Mighty in battle
      Father of the fatherless
30   Ever Faithful, Ever Sure
      The King of Glory,

Eternal Creator of all creatures,
Holy, Peaceful, Redeemer of the redeemed
The First without Equal
35   Almighty God of all creation. Selah

Jah Jehovah! Jah Jehovah! Jah Jehovah! Selah.

It's Spring Time

It's Spring Time
the dead shall spring up and shine
it's a rain of comfort,
time of healing and deliverance
5 creating a way where there was none,
germinating hope for the hopeless
generating light for the dark souls;
gracing the forgotten and the rejects

It's Spring time;
10 arise ye lukewarm spirit
receive My Power
today is your day of restoration
it's Spring time
Spring up and live.

It's Spring Time: Get up and live

Call Me

Part One

From the time of creation
I've given you Power and Authority
over all creatures
you were made by me
I've endowed you with my own Spirit
assured you, I am with you to the end time

Part Two

Anytime, anywhere, anyhow
you call upon me,
Lo, there; I am with you
even if you don't call upon me
my eyes follow you
wherever you go

Part Three

But you must invite me
If you need me
I cannot force my way into your life
I just can't
I cannot intrude;
cannot break my own rules

Part Four

What are you waiting for?
Why are you crying?
Why are you sitting down passively?
Why allow enemies to deride your situation?
Can Satan tear down your walls and break in?

Haven't I told you, be strong, be courageous

Part Five

Call me, by my pseudo name even now,
Invite me in momentarily
I shall come into your life
Turn your situation around.

My Plan for You

My plan for you
is good and just
to give you hope and future
a good accomplishment
5   for all your troubles

My desire for you
is to accomplish goodness
that I have ordained you for
a head and not the tail
10   above and not beneath

I have given you all you can ever need
I give you peace, perfect peace
It is well
With your body, spirit and soul.

My Plan for You: Beautiful and Good

Go for It

When I say
Go for it,
I want you to change your attitudes
you cannot get it the way you are
5   you just got to change your position

When I declare
go for it,
I know you can get it
I made you a Power container

10   When I command you
to go for it
you have no other option
than to heed My advice
you just have to go for it

15   No man-made laws,
can stop you from getting it,
no scientific explanations can hold you back,
no story, logic, reasoning, opinion, name
can void my word

20   I have commanded you to go for it
I made you a Prince, the King of all creation
nobody or anything can stop you
unless you want to stop yourself

Now, I say once again
25   No man-made law or proclamation
Can stop you
do not stop yourself
Just go and get it.

Go for it: Get it

The Judgment

Part One

Behold,
I saw the Son of man
seated in His glory
pronouncing judgment
on all nations not minding race or creed
I saw them being separated
sheep to the right
for His glory
goats to the left
for His eternal punishment

Part Two

Behold
I saw the dead
on land, sea, air and hell
small and great, old and young,
standing before the throne of judgment
with a mighty book opened
The Book of Life legibly printed on it,
from where came pronouncement

Part Three

Behold;
I saw death and hell
being thrown into the lake of fire,
with all those whose names were missing
the fornicators, liars, sorcerers,
idolaters, whoremongers, murderers,
thrown into the lake of sulphur burning fire

Part Four

Those rejoicing were exceedingly rejoicing
wailing wailers were gnashing their teeth
Hearing the pronouncements.

The Judgement: Peace or War

The Holy Communion

Eat and drink
my body and blood
I give to you
for I will not partake with you again
5   but in my Kingdom

Now;
It's time for the Last Supper
I give you my blood
I donate my body
10   a remission of sin

We shall sit round the table
to dine again in my Father's Kingdom
when
there will be no weeping, or sorrow
15   we shall rejoice for ever

Heavenly dew
is on those who eat it
no more death, sickness and affliction
theirs is liberty in Christ
20   freedom from all contaminants

Eat, be set free
drink, be loosed from all diseases
Afflicted, receive your freedom
Troubled souls, be at peace
25   your oil shall run over

This is my gift
to all believers
your spiritual eyes shall be opened
you shall behold my glory

30   My hidden treasures shall be revealed to you

     Drink and be filled with joy
     no dull moments, no wretchedness or failure
     drink this for your liberty
     my wisdom, knowledge and understanding
35   shall be added unto you

     Eat and live
     drink and see the glory of the Lord God
     it's the greatest nutrient
     an answer for your weary soul
40   drink and testify to my fullness

     Eat and drink
     not for the world's testament
     but for my truth
     I give myself to you
45   Give yourself to me.

The Holy Communion: Eat, drink till I return

Your Mindset

This is what you are
to yourself
If you think you can not
you will not
your mindset who you are
If you think you may
perhaps you will

Ability to do or not to do
Is within: inherent
If you profess success and good health
so shall it be
nobody can give it to you
are you ready to receive it?
you must be determined to receive
you must have a right mindset

Stop blaming it on your birthplace
your stars, root, your family or someone else
yes, they may be limiting factors
but are not strong enough
to prevent you from getting it
your mindset is what must be right

Weakness is what He used most
David defeated Goliath with a right attitude
Isaac did not question God at his old age
Jacob became blessed: from nothing to
Joseph was kind to his famished brothers

To be a conqueror, champion an overcomer
You must have the right mindset.

Your mindset: Your life's barometer

A Dead Branch

Part One

I gave them
Power and Authority
over all contrary Spirit
over all demon and disease
over sorrow, pain and affliction
I licensed them
to preach My Good News to all
to heal, recover, possess and restore
to shame, release and bind
in My name

Part Two

I assured them
where there is My Word
there is power, hope, liberty and joy
authority to shut and open
bound and release
punish, award and reward
through My name
I enthroned them over the work of my hands
proclaimed them Gods
yet, they seek after graven images

Part Three

What did they do?
Who did they run to?
religious cankerworms and termites
acrimonious praise, unclean prayerful hearts
bitter division and religious bigotries
in my own House of Praise

dictating to My Spirit how to operate
scheming for earthly materialism
pretending to serve me, the *Jehovah Nissi*
The Maker of the Spirit man

Part Four

They claim to be mine
yet don't know who they serve
they swear in my name
their spirit mortgaged to their familiar spirit
I gave them power but they remain powerless
like an empty drum with dreadful noise
they can't heal, release or bind
sucked in and held captive by contrary spirit
bound by the depths of their waywardness
held captive by fear, deceits of their hearts

Part Five

I called, warned and sent them words
they refused to contrite their hearts
'cause of their evil deeds
their congregation leave in droves
my prophets feel unperturbed
elders wallowing in adultery and incest
youths' passion for money is unquenchable
past visioners manufactured the-Lord-said
yet claiming to be serving the true God
hoping to receive from the King of Kings

Part Six

I gave them Power
they see no vision, speak no more in tongues
their children dream but nightmares

their elders mourn their good old days
recounting the lost glory of the past
which brings healing and joy no more?
I speak but don't listen to my voice again
they formulate visions and lack wisdom
forged dreams and have no understanding
buy miracles from the power of Darkness

Part Seven

No peace, no healing, no faith, no deliverance
highly religious and brutally ceremonious
tormented by their shadows
for seeking after self-justification
caressing their hearts' desires
misrepresenting the Word of God
following their hearts' dictates
flowing in mundane experience
stealing from me, the *Jehovah Jireh*
knowing the truth but still held in chains

Part Eight

See, I am coming, coming, sooner than later
like a thief at dawn
Judgment will come first to my house
to those who claimed to be mine
I am no respecter of persons
all dead branches shall be uprooted
gathered for fire to bud no more
I am the Vine Keeper
I have spoken
Mark my word.

A Dead Branch: Good for fire

His Gifting

The Almighty Father
Giver of all good things
Faith, Revelation, and Prophesying
to serve and honour
the Trinity

Custodian of five ministries
Apostle, Prophet, Evangelist, Pastor, Teacher
to nurture and equip the church
never with arrogance, pride or jealousy
for edification of the body of Christ

Lord God,
bless me with your Holy Spirit
one Lord, one faith, one baptism
God above all, through all and in all
all good gifts come from the Lord above

If you lack
please ask and you shall be given
to profit, to save, to edify
not for safe-keeping or show-off
or on the shelves for putrefaction

Lord's gifting
are according to measure of faith
through Christ the Son
at the instance of the Holy Spirit
never moved by sentiments

He gives as He pleases without recrimination
God's giftings
are without repentance

        they bring peace, joy, and restoration
30   To true believers.

A Fulfiled Life

To live a fulfilled life;
I will think positively and fruitfully
forgive and forget
love and be compassionate

5   For love and peace to be
I need to kill the fire of anger, ill feeling
life's journey a smooth, a slippery
won't be held hostage by the past
see today an opportunity for tomorrow's joy

10   Nobody was born an idiot,
the society creates one
I'll learn from the past mistakes
see disappointment as a learning curve
give God His space and grace

15   I will stop complaining and be responsible
reduce professing misery and misfortune,
affirm greatness and life to the full
show gratitude for every little thing
be completely focused on what I do
20   guard my thoughts, actions and companions

Be open to all possibilities
conceptualise and see myself in my new role
of a fulfiled life
will live a life of fullness
25   And a fulfiling one.

Fulfiled Life: Is contented

A Good Friendship

Part One

Tell me about a friend
and I will show you
the meaning of a good friendship
a friend, when visiting
wants to be treated like a guest
a good friend treats you like a guest
in your own home

Part Two

A friend assures you of his affectionate love
a good friend wipes away your tears,
lends you his shoulder to cry upon
and more compassionate with your feeling
a friend can forget your landmark,
a good friend does not only remind you of it
but also leaves a lasting impression

Part Three

A friend brings you a rose flower
a good friend helps water your rose garden
a friend keeps the friendship
for what he gets out of it
a good friend gives you all
but ask nothing in return

Part Four

A friend talks with you about his problems
a good friend stirs you on the right path
should problem come

you are in it together

Part Five

A friend will call you the next day
to find out why you were in a foul state
a good friend will not go home
without finding out the cause of your anxiety

Part Six

A friend will still keep some secrets from you
a good friend will share everything with you

My dear friend,
don't tell me about a friend
please, be
A good friend.

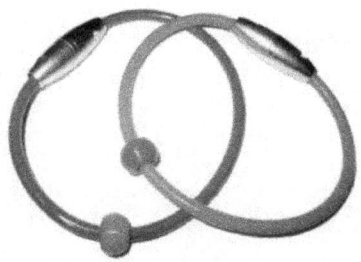

A Good Friendship: Not For Sale

Use Me

Part One

Holy Spirit
use me for your honour
Holy Spirit
fill me with your power
Holy Spirit anoint my lips
let me speak of God's glory
I need your Power to
fill me and cover me

Part Two

Holy Spirit
I am hungry for you
feed me with the heavenly bread
I shall be hungry no more
use me for your honour
set me on fire
work inside me
Till I am made whole.

Guide Me

Part One

Guide me, guide me, guide me
lead me, lead me, lead me
hold me, hold me, hold me
on my journey through
shield me, bless me, fortify me
In your sanctify
Your light unto my path
Your love into my heart
Your word into my soul
Your peace into my spirit man

Part Two

Guide me, guide me, guide me
lead me, lead me, lead me
hold me, hold me, hold me
on my journey through
shield me, fortify me, bless me
touch me, mould, heal me
lead me into your sanctuary
Your power shall rest upon me
Your healing I need
Your divine will shall see me through.

Faithful Saviour

Part One

My life I give to you
It's only You I know
I will obey you my Lord
In your word I find solace
My trust is in you
Come, faithful Saviour
Into my life

Part Two

Faithful Saviour
You are the Lord of my life
My Captain, my King, my Father
Faithful Saviour
Gracious and Merciful Friend
I surrender all to You
You are my Anchor.

Fill me O Lord

Part One

When I am down and miserable
fill me O Lord
when I am sick and at the point of death
fill me O lord
when I am confused and confounded
fill me O lord
when I am persecuted and attacked
fill me O Lord

Part Two

Fill me, fill me, fill me
heal me, heal me, heal me
bless me, bless me, bless me
mould me, mould me, mould me
use me, use me, use me
free me, free me, free me
lead me, lead me, lead me,
when I am down and miserable
Fill me, fill me, fill me O Lord.

Your Disciple

Part One

I am a disciple of God
commissioned by the Father
through His Son
to preach the Good New
and proclaim the Lord's Second coming

Part Two

I am a disciple of God
with power to bind and loose
a light to the blind
a way to the Father
through the Son

Part Three

 I am your disciple
commissioned by the Father
through His Son
to preach the Gospel
Make disciples among nations.
.

In Your loving arms

Your love for me is immeasurable
Your plan for me is wonderful
the fellowship unprecedented
my rebellion creates a separation
my thought, my action, my reaction
became an abomination
brought for me
generational shame, curse and death
consequence of my unfaithfulness

Your extraordinary love for me
through Your only begotten Son
brought for me with your precious blood
generational unmerited favour and mercy
Back into my Father's loving arms.

What is Life

Part One

What is Life?
but a ship on the high Sea
sailing on a journey
not knowing how long, how well or how rough
tempest roars, lighting strikes
only determines to reach her destination

Life never measured by the volume of wealth
nor by the amount of knowledge gained
life is not the jewelleries or properties bequit
never on the heavy bank account
nor the priceless documents or artefacts
 in the security vault

Part Two

Fulfilled Life is adjudged
by beautiful clothes put on the naked
shelter built over heads of the poor
bread provided for the motherless
hope created for the rejected
compassion brought to the persecuted
quality advice given to the confused
by the hands of friendship extended
when it was difficult to do so
lamp shown on people's feet
light beamed on to their path
quality of knowledge passed on
meritorious services to people and God
whilst still in the ship on Life

Part Three

These are what people will remember you by
The legacy, the heritage, the testimonies
will outlive you even when you are long gone

Part Four

What is Life?
a ship on the high Sea
sailing on a journey
not knowing how long, how well or how rough
tempest roars, lighting strikes
Must reach her destination someday.

What is Life: A ship on sail

I Will Make Heaven

Part One

I know that my Covenant lives
what a relief for me
He lives for ever more
ambassador of His I am
minister of His Kingdom
to represent His interest here
speak with authority
proclaim the Good News
throughout my sojourn here
while my lamp burns

Part Two

A citizen of Heavenly Kingdom
redeemed from the beginning of creation
His will, not mine, will prevail
I am His, without Him, I am nothing
the three hundred and sixty-five secrets
I surrender all to Him
my home is not made by mortal hands
I will make it back home
to live for ever with my Covenant
in my eternal home

Part Three

Where there is no pressure
with the Eternal One
Behind the Clouds.

I Will Make Heaven: I will be there

Epilogue

Behold from behind the clouds came a thundering voice like the roaring of the ocean, and I saw a mighty hand came from the sky and stretched forth unto me, holding a gigantic scroll with an inscription written on it; *the 365 Secrets of A Fulfilled Life,* and the thundering voice said unto me, *take, read, write, share and spread it till I come back for the glorious Millennium Reign.*

www.ingramcontent.com/pod-product-compliance
Lightning Source LLC
Chambersburg PA
CBHW032302150426
43195CB00008BA/546